An Invisible Girl

An Invisible Girl

by

Judy Young

© 2020 Judy Young. All rights reserved.
This material may not be reproduced in any form, published,
reprinted, recorded, performed, broadcast,
rewritten or redistributed without
the explicit permission of Judy Young.
All such actions are strictly prohibited by law.

Cover design by Shay Culligan

Cover photograph by IIona Panych

ISBN: 978-1-950462-90-2

Kelsay Books Inc.

kelsaybooks.com

502 S 1040 E, A119
American Fork, Utah 84003

To Ross,
with love

Judy

Contents

Always	11
English	13
Music	16
A Cat Has Nine	18
Group Project	20
Coveted Prizes	24
Speech and Debate	25
Art	28
Saturday	30
Happy Sixteenth Birthday	33
Driver's License	36
Red Light, Green Light	38
History	40
Forever Cognizant	42
Geometry	44
Red	46
Bits and Pieces	48
Foreign Language Credits	51
Human Development	56
Journalism	58
P.E.	62
Just Before Suppertime	63
Thoughts for My Mother	67
Either One	68
School Play	70
Graduation	72

so vivid and real
in this dream I touch, see, smell
but can't awaken

Always

My friends came—
Quieted by unfamiliar surroundings,
Hesitant in the open doorway.
They stood
Backlit by the brilliant fluorescence of sterility
Which invaded the room,
An impersonal attempt to clean away
The smudge of dimness that hovered around me,
Where fears grow in corners,
Breeding on obscurity
As infectious as the diseases
That permeate these rooms.
The light's starkness intruded
Upon the veiled faces in the room,
Momentarily exposing reality
Before the door swung shut once more.

My mother thought it might help—
I might recognize my friends.
In her panicked imagination,
She saw them
Rambunctiously and jovially
Barging into the room
As if from the halls of school.

Vivacious adolescents with the lucid light of life,
They would pull me from the black abyss,
Rescue me with long ropes of their braids,
Like Rapunzel from their not yet relinquished childhoods,
Letting down their hair so I could climb the golden plaits
And resist the curse placed upon me,

Thus following the path of all childhood tales
Where the fair young maiden is saved
From a tragic fate cast upon her unsuspectedly
By an unknown demon.

My friends came—
Three of them.
They stood by my bed,
Shoulder to shoulder,
Drawn to my side reluctantly
Yet with the insistent magnetic force of curiosity.
Stiffly, they stared down at me
For a few moments that lasted their lifetimes,
Looking down at the blue pools of my eyes
That reflected nothing back.

I scared them.
They cried.
I cried also
But no one knew.
My mother was right.
I remembered them, and they,
They would now remember me,
Always.

English

First day of school.
Assignment:
Write a paper about you,
Who you are,
What makes you you.
Use two quotes that describe
Your inner self.

The trouble is
I don't know who I am.
I can only look in the mirror,
Describe what I see.
What you see.
The outer me.

Blue eyes.
Baby blue.
Chicory blue.
Blue as the summer's sky
Reflected in fluid pools
That absorb the world around me.
These pools sparkle,
Mischievously laugh and dance.
They are shallow.
They mirror what you want to see.
But below the glittery sun-speckled surface
Lie midnight hues,
Deep and impenetrable,
Where I reflect upon what these pools absorb.
Their infinite depths
I am still trying to explore.

Blonde hair.
Strawberry blonde.
Honey blonde.
Gilded threads giving golden opportunities
To sparkle in the sun,
Shimmer in a breeze.
I am shiny and fresh,
Bouncing with enthusiasm,
Seeking attention, showing off.
I long to be touched.
But, like Frost said,
Nothing gold can stay.
I become unmanageable,
Dull, uninviting
And sullen,
Wishing to be left alone.

Thin body.
Pencil thin.
Thin as a rail.
Merely skin and bones.
There is no meat to me.
I bury my thoughts,
Exposing only a shadow of myself.
Hiding,
Pretending,
Afraid to do anything but follow.
I need to fatten up these delicate feelings,
This thin skinned
Lack of confidence.

Who am I?
I don't know who I am.

Emily Dickinson wrote,
I'm nobody
Who are you?
Are you nobody, too?

No.
I am not nobody.

I am anybody.
Am I you?
Could you possibly be me, too?

Music

It was always the four of us,
A quartet,
Inseparable.
We could have been a double set
Of conjoined twins
Moving as a whole
Through play groups,
Then kindergarten and elementary,
Finally reaching middle school.
Oh, we were so cool,
Always singing the same song,
Never deviating from each other.

And now, here we are in high school.
What on Earth could cause us to separate,
Now, after all those years?
We worry about life after high school
When we must undergo this operation,
Cut the binds that hold us together.
School is our shared skin.
We can't imagine what that life,
Which still seems so distant
Yet is steadily creeping upon us, will bring.

We fear we must become individuals.
Individuality—we have fought against this for so long,
Checking with each other,
Consulting about the appropriateness
And seeking the approval
Of all our actions,
Our hair,
Our clothes,
Our thoughts.

So, we have made a pact
Not to let time be the scalpel
Which cuts us apart.
But we know
Deep within our collective souls,
One of us will be the first
To be severed.

A Cat Has Nine

I live two lives,
Or maybe three
Or do I live as many as the people I know,
Each seeing in me what they want to see?
How can I ever expect to know who I am
When there is no consensus from the masses?

I am the daughter,
Confusing and frustrating in a father's eyes,
A simile in a mother's.
I am a sister,
Competitive rival from birth
Over love, attention, power.
I am the smart one,
The one with academic prowess and potential.
But whose student am I?
The English teacher sees me as a fledgling author—
Her influence will be mentioned in dedications.
But within the school day, I become
The science teacher's cure for cancer,
The coach's Olympic athlete.

Everyone is vying over who I am
And even within myself
I am inconsistent, unstable.
I want to be the clown,
Center of attention,
But when it is given
I shy away.

I want to be compassionate,
Everybody's friend and confidante,
The one who will quietly listen,
Give silent support,
But when someone comes to my door
I don't let them in.

I portray indifference toward those I care for the most
And attend to those who interest me least.
I seek friendship and companionship
But select isolation and solitude.
My shyness is taken for conceit,
My assertiveness scares me.
I am my own enigma.

Group Project

I felt your eyes on me,
Staring from the front of the class,
But I tried to be invisible,
My head lowered,
Eyes on my opened book.
Could you read me like one,
Knowing that I had not read the assignment,
Not this time?
There are others who never complete their work.
Do they feel your eyes?
Or do you not waste your glances on them—
It won't do any good?
But why not give me a break,
Turn your eyes away from me?
I am usually prepared,
Just not today.

We had made our plans,
Worked out all the details.
A school night of freedom and fun.

There was a group project.
No one would question that.
We have always been so responsible . . .
I'll be at her house, she'll be at yours,
He'll be at mine, you'll be at his . . .
Where does the circle begin or end?
No one will know.

We met at the park.
We raced like children,
The boys chasing the girls,
Sliding down the slides,
Swinging toward the stars,
Twirling dizzily on the merry-go-round,
Laughing and frolicking in our freedom.

I knew you would be there.
I had watched you,
Dreamt about you,
But I had carefully painted myself invisible.

I felt your eyes on me,
Staring at the back of my head,
But I thought I was invisible,
My head lowered,
Eyes on my opened book.
Can you read my thoughts,
Knowing that I cannot concentrate on the assignment,
Not this time?
My attention is solely on you.
I can feel your eyes,
They are not wasted glances,
They make me feel so good.
But why can't I show my feelings,
Turn my eyes your way?
I am usually confident,
But not today.

You unexpectedly reached for my hand,
Leading me away,
And I followed,
Away from the others at the playground,
Quickly running, racing,
Twisting through a grove of trees.
We slowed our pace,
Strolling through the patchwork of light
That fell through the leaves,
Dappling the lawn
As breezes softly caressed the trees
And whispered a moonlight sonata.

I thought you would kiss me,
Your lips would touch mine
Under the magnificent star-filled skies.
But you didn't.

We slowly walked on.
We started talking and I realized
I had never spoken before.
These were my first true words.
My words.
Interwoven with yours.
They were threads
Made of dreams and desires,
Fears and philosophies.
They wove seductive patterns between our minds
As, for the first time,
I allowed myself to be known.

I felt your eyes on me,
Staring from the back of the room.
But this time I will not paint myself invisible.
I raised my head,
My eyes moved from my opened book.
Can you read my feelings,
Knowing that I will not hide them,
Not this time?
I can feel your eyes on me,
They look deep inside me
Trespassing into my heart,
But I am not shying away.
I turn my eyes your way.
I have been invisible,
But not today.

Coveted Prizes

Downplayed excitement,
Feigned indifference,
Rushed through the halls.
An electricity
Barely perceptible
Behind masked faces.

Jocular pushing and shoving,
Teasing about who needs it,
Boasting and bragging,
No one admitting they don't already know it all.

But secretly, everyone was enthusiastic.
No one took it lightly.
No one ignored it.
There were none scattered
Like leaf litter after a storm.
None on the floors,
In the trash,
Left on desks
Like the fate of brochures and leaflets
Distributed by the guidance counselor
Or health teacher.
These all went home.
Coveted prizes.

I was no different.
I could hardly wait
To open
The most important book in my life,
Published by
The Department of Motor Vehicles.

Speech and Debate

What?
We have to give a two-minute speech?
Impromptu?
How could he just spring
Something like this on us?
We have ten minutes to prepare!
Doesn't he know anything?

I got up late this morning.
I didn't have time to wash my hair.
I can't stand up there with my hair
Looking like this.
I could pull it back,
It would look better,
But I left it down
Because, if I hold my head just right,
It will hang over
This big zit on my forehead.
Pulling my hair back is out of the question.
I'll just have to get lower marks
Because of improper speech giving posture.

And this shirt.
Can I go to my locker?
I need to get my jacket.
Because I need it.
Please?

I wore this shirt just to appease my mother.
It looks cute on you.
Just put it on.
You don't have time to argue.
You should have gotten up earlier.
Just what I want to do,

Stand up there looking cute.
Please, please let me get my jacket?

Look at her.
Standing there like a magazine model.
Why can't I be like her?
Her hair is perfect,
The perfect color,
Every hair in the right place.
She has never had a zit
On her perfect face
That holds beautiful eyes,
High cheekbones,
Just the right amount of blush,
Lips that form the perfect smile
Under the perfect nose,
Around the perfectly straight, white teeth.
Her clothes always fit,
Are always the latest styles
And even the girls can't keep their eyes off
Her perfect body.
She stands up there
In front of everyone
One hundred percent confident
In her ability
To exude beauty.

My turn?
I have to follow her?
Two minutes of pure torture.
Then I slump back to my seat
And others shuffle forward,
Taking their turns,
Until all have been publicly humiliated.

My grade?
Ninety-five percent.
Perfect,
Except for your posture.
Stand up straight next time.

That's all?
Just my posture?
No other input?
I'd like to debate
But he turns away from me
Telling her
She had nothing to say.
He wants to see her after class.
Figures.
She always gets all the attention.

Art

Your perspective is off.
You need to focus on a point
Far off on the horizon.
From every other place,
All will somehow be
In relationship to that point.

Remember to keep things
In proportion.
Things may seem big,
Sometimes too big,
Because they are close to you.
Don't forget the small things—
The details.
What is in the background
Can be dwarfed by the immensity
Of the foreground,
But they are what make the piece
Interesting.

Make sure you look at your world—
Really see it
For what it is.
Grass is not green,
The sky is not blue.
There are thousands of hues, tints.
What values do you have?
Are you trying out new ideas,
Mixing new colors,
Seeing through others' eyes?

Think about your composition,
Your positioning and placement.
There is both positive space
And negative space,
Which takes on its own shapes,
Its own importance.

Don't assume
That things will work out the way you want on their own—
Balance in art rarely just happens.
You have to be in control
To create harmony amongst all the elements.

Saturday

Arm across shoulder,
Arm across shoulder,
Left foot crossing right,
Right foot crossing left,

In unison,
Four abreast down the sidewalk
We walk,
Ponytails bouncing and eyes sparkling.

Men, empty handed, smile,
Women laden with bags
And children's hands, scowl,
Stepping off the curb to go around us.

We giggle along,
Stopping to gaze at dreams on posters
Outside the theatre,
Then dart into dress shops

Holding up wedding dresses,
Prom dresses,
Negligees,
Bras with size D cups.

We zip into the candy store,
Emerging with silly grins
Under wax teeth
And luscious lips,

Laughing at our four windowed reflections,
Sticking out our tongues at another group of girls
Who walk by with sneers and rolled eyes,
Too sophisticated to have fun.

To escape the eyes of boys
Who spied our stuck-out tongues,
We barge rambunctiously
Into the nearest doorway

Rushing into the quiet office
Of the startled insurance salesman,
Apologetically tripping over each other
To fall back out onto the sidewalk

In front of the boys who follow us
Into a variety store,
Flipping through magazines
With muffled control,

Self-conscious heads down,
Female to female giggling,
Female to male eye contact,
Male to male jostling, elbowing.

We leave, they follow,
But not into the toy store,
Where we try out teddy bear chairs,
Talking about the boys,

Then forgetting them.
Moving into the gift shop,
We read cards to each other
Instead of buying them,

Then wander out into the sunny sidewalk.
We reach the end of the shopping center
As we reach the end
Of our Saturday afternoon,

Sitting on the curb, waiting for our ride,
Shoulder to shoulder, legs outstretched,
Left ankle over right ankle,
Left ankle over right ankle.

Happy Sixteenth Birthday

Happy Birthday, Daughter!
May All Your Dreams and Wishes Come True!
With all our love,
Mom and Dad

Dreams and wishes.
All my dreams and wishes.

Dreams and wishes used to be so easy.
I'd dream of fairylands and princesses,
Beautiful pastel colors,
Soft, sunny days.
Rainbows and magic.
Unicorns.

I'd ride behind my love
On a dappled gray stallion,
My long silk dress flowing
As we galloped to our castle
Where happily ever after was
Unquestionably obtainable.

I floated like dandelion fluff
Up amongst the stars
I wished upon,
Knowing all my wishes
Would come true,
Just as the toys
And shiny party shoes
With taps on the toes
Appeared in wrapped boxes
After blowing out the candles.

But dreams and wishes don't come so easy any more.
Dreams overlap with wondering,
Confuse themselves with goals,
Mix themselves with fears.
Wishes merge with needs.
Possibilities compete with probabilities.
Nothing is unquestionably obtainable.

I dream of friendship
Pure and loyal
And of love,
Sincere and lasting.
I wish to be accepted,
Long to be included.
I have dreams,
Wishes,
Wonderings,
Goals
For the future.

But I watch television
Where dreams and wishes
Vanish with reality,

Violence and war
Are not rectified
By a knight in shining armor.
Haunting eyes reveal wishes
Won't grant freedom
From poverty and disease.
Death haunts my dreams
And I am terrified.
I can think of nothing worse.

I know that all my dreams and wishes
Can't come true.
But will any of them?

Driver's License

Here I am.
All laid out
On this little plastic card
Three and three-eighths by two and one-fourth inches
Containing all you need to know of me.

Name
Address
Social Security number
Gender
Date of Birth
Height
Weight
Eye color
Even my picture—
Proof that it is me.

My card of freedom.
My card of independence.
My card of responsibility.
I am maturing,
Nearing adulthood.

Stamped across the front
Will not be 21 until . . .
Is this a guarantee?

On the back,
Medical alert.
I have nothing to be alert about.
Gift giving information.
An anatomical gift
Upon my death.
They want to know if I will

Give my liver,
My kidneys,
My heart . . .
I have to sign that I will
Donate my body.

Of course, I will do this.
But not yet.
I will not think of this now.
I am not old enough
To have to think
Of this.

Red Light, Green Light

There's not much to do here,
In this town,
Or any town, probably.
We gather
Like moths under the street lamp,
Our meeting spot
Where nights,
Warm and languid,
Slowly pass by.

This was the base for our childhood games.
Flashlight Tag.
Hide and Seek.
Red Light, Green Light.

We still play.
We gather like moths.
You're it.
You spot me
Though you have left your flashlight at home.
We run away to hide
Together
In the old favorite place
Back behind the shed
Where no one can spot us,
Crawling into the space
Made by the roses that hang their petaled heads
Over the fence in front of us.
We sit giggling quietly
Like we did when children,
Side by side,
Shoulders touching,
Nothing but the moon—
Our green light

Shining through the leaves
That dance with their shadows.

I have never been aware
Of our space
Until tonight
When together we become quiet.
I feel your shoulder
Touching mine.
The length of your arm
Lies next to mine.
Your knee, mine.
I feel the silence,
As fragrant as the roses.
Your breath, mine.
Your heart, mine.
Mine is racing
Afraid you will,
Afraid you won't.
You turn slightly
And I follow.
Your lips, mine,
As the moon shines
Through the roses,
Through the leaves,
Red light,
Green light.

History

History and my mother are the same—
Both repeat themselves.

I sit in history and wonder
About the past.
Did Columbus' mother complain
About maps scattered all over the floor?
Did Henry VIII's mother
Repeat over and over,
Try, try again?
Gutenberg was probably constantly reminded
To wash his inky hands.
Newton's mother harped on and on,
Don't just sit there,
Watching them fall,
Start picking!
Were the ancients
Told not to stay out late
Stargazing?

I tried and tried again
To get his attention,
Mapping out in my head
Where I would accidentally
Run into him
But I finally washed my hands of him.
He didn't seem to notice me.
I just sat there in history class,
Spirits falling,
Until the bell rang.
Then, picking up my books,
I told my friends he was history.

But I didn't mean it.
I wanted history to repeat itself.
I wanted to feel his arm on my shoulder,
I wanted his lips to touch mine again,
And again.

That night,
I found out my history teacher was right.
History does repeat itself,
And so does my mother
Reminding me it is a school night
As he and I left to go stargazing.

Forever Cognizant

There for the grace of God go I.
What in the world does that mean?
It's my mother's expression.
She uses expressions like this
Frequently.
Most are somehow connected
With lectures
But this one,
This one is different.

This one is a prayer,
A plea
Whispered in desperation,
A verbal amulet
Warding off
Demons and devastations.
When repeated, it reduces risks,
Removes possibilities.
Both sword and shield
It is also her prayer of gratitude,
Of thanksgiving,
A verbal offering
To both thank and appease the fates,
Letting them know that she is aware
And forever cognizant
That she has been spared once again.
My mother recites this expression
Ritualistically,
Superstitiously,
And I mock her utterance.
But what if it's not untrue,

What if she forgot
To repeat the incantation
Just one time?
My mother takes no such chances.
She wants no relationship
To a sacrificial lamb.

Geometry

Theorem: If only I would have . . .
Proof: I will never know.

Geometry is the study of lines.
Lines are infinite.
Rays start at a given point, continuing in one direction.
Segments have a start point and an end point.
Two lines that intersect form an angle.

Lives are not lines.
I thought mine was
Until today.
I was heading toward infinity,
Mortality was the essence
Of other people's lines—
I didn't connect it with mine.
Today started out as a ray,
A ray of sunshine,
A ray of promise for the future,
Stretching out forever in front of me.

My ray.
Starting point: school.
Headed down Sunshine Avenue.
Someone else started another ray
Somewhere else,
Traveling on a perpendicular line.
Our lines intersected
At a given point
Forming an angle.

It was not the angle
I was expecting.
It wasn't right.
I had been too obtuse to see the possibility
That left me in this acute state.
If I were in physics class
I could tell you about velocity
And actions
That produce equal and opposite reactions.
But I am in geometry
And I have just completed
The unit on segments.

Red

Red is my color.
Red has drawn itself to me
And flows though my life.

Red rattles,
Red booties.
Red dances above me,
Raggedy Ann faces with bright yarn hair,
Flashy and glittery smiles
Reflecting in my infant eyes.

Red balloons,
Red lollipops.
Red covers my feet
As patent leather party shoes
Pump high against the sky,
Swing low across the ground.

Red apples,
Red crayons.
Red brushes my cheek
As my ribboned braids
Bounce and skip with me
Down the drive to meet the school bus.

Red kickballs,
Red paint.
Red spreads across my shoulder,
And stretches down my arm
As I don a hooded cape,
Star of the third grade play.

Red pencils,
Red corrections.

Red adorns my shirt,
Acknowledging second place
After spelling scarlet
But missing sanguine.

Red dress,
Red valentines.
Red pierces my heart
With the rose's thorn
Because it came from my father
And not the boy I dreamt of.

Red lipstick,
Red nail polish.
Red burns my face
Uncontrollably
As a boy's lips
First brush mine.

Red car,
Red stop sign.
Red lights pump high against the sky.
Red dances above me
Flashy and glittery,
Reflecting in my uncomprehending eyes.

Red fluid,
Red blood.
Red brushes my cheek and burns my face,
Red spreads across my shoulder and stretches down my arm,
Red adorns my shirt and covers my feet.
Red pierces my heart.

Bits and Pieces

I am a piece in a kaleidoscope—
My world twisting,
Spinning.
Bright lights, faces,
In and out,
Nothing registers,
Nothing clicks.
Confusion.
Twisting.
Spinning.
Falling.

Close your eyes,
Just close your eyes.
Let the kaleidoscope
Slide you away,
Away from the present.
Twist it and see
Bits of the past,
Comforting pieces
That lean against each other,
Fall into place.
There is nothing special
In this montage,
Just a collection of pieces—
A colorful mishmash
That when put together and mixed,
Form new and beautiful shapes,
Something to focus on,
Bright and wondrous
Bits of life.

Feet dangle white above the green grass
With a splash of sun catching droplets
The sprinkler glittered on rocks
Kicked all the way down the street
To the park where the slide was so high,
As high as the kite soaring over a sand castle
Washed by waves of the vast sun-diamonded sea.

Give it another twist,
Just keep your eyes shut,
Open only your mind
As you fly, no hands, following tar lines in the road,
Legs reddened by the sun, or maybe cold wind.
Coast along the sidewalk squares,
Clickety, clickety, clickety,
The train's rhythm, crickets,
Curtains flapping in cool breezes,
Sounds of open-windowed nights.
Follow a bluebird, dart like a hummingbird,
Past the checker board
Where Grandpa sits in the shade
Watching you roll down the bank,
Arms to your sides, rolling, rolling,
The world green and blue, green and blue.

Twist the kaleidoscope.
Your smile, your beautiful smile,
The infectious one that shines with mine
Like a double rainbow shining through icicles
Or between the new green field and the purple skies
Bringing the smells of French lilacs
Dropping white petals

As soft as the touch of the piano,
Spreading its song like ripples
Of a leaf dropping on water.

The hotness of sand heats outstretched arms
Making angels in the snow
Ice-cream drops into root beer
And foams over the lip as my horse gallops
Through the green that covers my eyes
When I pull the dryer-warmed sweatshirt
Over my head, soft as pussy willows
In my grandmother's bright yellow kitchen.
Sunlight streaming through rippling waters,
Stepping stone to stone
Tripping, falling backwards,
Falling into more shapes,
Colors, brights, darks, mosaic
Kaleidoscopic bits and pieces
Of my life.

Foreign Language Credits

I have to take two years
Of a foreign language.
Spanish, Greek, Latin?
Which would be the best?
Which would help me through my life?
Will I ever need a foreign language?

I chose Spanish, *Español*.
Señor Profesor
Lost me on the first day
Down a street in a village in Spain.
He said he wanted us to feel
The reality of another world.

Señor Profesor dice
Usted se sentirá como en su casa
Cuando usted entiende lo que dicen.

Señor Profesor dice,
"By totally immersing you each day,
You will become part
Of this other world,
Not alienated from it.
At the end of the year,
You will have found your way
Around the village.
Your world will be expanded,
Encompassing and owning
Both worlds."

Señor Profesor dice
Usted se sentirá como en su casa
Cuando usted entiende lo que dicen.

Señor Profesor dice,
"It is all a trick of language.
What we comprehend,
What we accept as reality,
What scares us,
What comforts us."

I began to comprehend
Little by little.

First colors—
Rojo, red.
Negro, black.
Blanco, white.

Then simple nouns—
Amigos, friends
Familia, family
Escuela, school.

And verbs—
Hablar, to talk.
Mirar, to watch.

Señor Profesor dice
Usted se sentirá como en su casa
Cuando usted entiende lo que dicen.

Soon we were putting words together,
Stringing unfamiliar sounds
Into comprehendible combinations.
Señor Professor
Kept taking us deeper and deeper
Into the village,

Into the foreign world,
And individual words
Began to stand out,
Blatantly obvious
Amongst the verbal noise.

Señor Profesor dice
Usted se sentirá como en su casa
Cuando usted entiende lo que dicen.

Then my village went black.
Negro.
And I awoke to bright lights.
Blanco.
What was this color,
Rojo,
That seemed to be flooding
This world,
This foreign world?

I am trying to grasp
The reality of this other world.
I see *mi familia*
And *mis amigos*
But I am not at *escuela*—
I am not in the village
Of *Señor Profesor's* classroom.

They want me to talk.
No hablo.
I can only watch,
Solamente miro,
The *blanco* lights
Before they turn *negro* again.

Señor Profesor dice
Usted se sentirá como en su casa
Cuando usted entiende lo que dicen.

I have been immersed
Once again into a foreign village.
But I don't recognize the words—
I don't understand what they say to each other,
What they say to my parents.
My parents have been immersed also,
They too have been dropped into this village.
They stare blankly, uncomprehendingly,
At these strangers from this other world.

Señor Profesor dice
Usted se sentirá como en su casa
Cuando usted entiende lo que dicen.

I am lost
Down a street in a village
Where no one is talking the same language.
I am not at home.
It sounds Greek to me,
Hematoma, cephalic, parietal cortex . . .

Put it in plain English
I hear my father say.
They have switched languages on him also.
They are not speaking English,
Or even Spanish.
Is it Latin?
Maybe I should have taken Latin.
But they say Latin is a dead language.

Señor Profesor dice
Usted se sentirá como en su casa
Cuando usted entiende lo que dicen.

Señor Profesor dice,
"It is all a trick of language.
What we comprehend,
What we accept as reality,
What scares us,
What comforts us."

Usted se sentirá como en su casa:
You will be at home

Cuando usted entiende lo que dicen:
When you understand what they say.

Señor Profesor dice
Usted se sentirá como en su casa
Cuando usted entiende lo que dicen.

Human Development

One by one
Off the list
They are checked
While anxious parents observe
Primitive reflexes
Recognizes faces
Lifts head
Smiles
Sits
Walks
Talks

They are taken for granted.
Indicators of intact neurological functioning
Signs of social affect
Evidence of emotionality
Responses to extrinsic environment
Confirmation of intrinsic impressions
Proof of mental processes

Milestones
Components of human life
Milestones

Proof of mental processes
Confirmation of intrinsic impressions
Response to extrinsic environment
Evidence of emotionality
Signs of social affect
Indicators of intact neurological functioning
They are taken for granted.

Talks
Walks
Sits
Smiles
Lifts head
Recognizes faces
Primitive reflexes
While anxious parents observe
They are checked
Off the list
One by one

Journalism

Headlines shout!
Read it! Read it!
Read all about it
While it's hot off the press!
It won't last long!

I was selected
To be one of the elite,
One of the journalism staff.
Usually you apply for this position
By submissions of papers
And grades
To a panel of teachers
And a board of other journalism students.
But I didn't go the regular route—
I bypassed the selection committee,
And yet
I became an integral part
Of gathering facts,
Writing the story.
My story.
My byline.

Headlines screamed out the news:
What happened?
Who?
Where?
When?
Facts.
My story
Was written.
A leading story,

Leading the curious to the scene.
Leading the readers to more questions.

How?
Why?

My follow-up story was written,
Stating more facts,
Clarifying accounts,
Quoting sources,
Discarding rumors.

And an editorial
Brought up more questions,
Thought provoking questions
Focusing on speculation,
Making judgments,
Offering opinions,
Expressing concerns.

My human interest story came next,
Following my parents,
My family,
My friends,
Bringing the event to everyone's heart,
Opening up emotions,
Empathy,
Sympathy,
And leading readers to both
Fear and relief
That it could have
And didn't
Happen to them.

The community poured over every word,
Their reading like a quiet vigil,
A show of support,
Yet also an obsessive need
To comprehend the incomprehensible,
A longing to know,
Feel,
Understand
The physical and emotional pain
Yet allowing them to be
Appreciative that they live
Without experiencing it.

Ads were run
By the red cross,
By citizen watchdog groups
Advocating changes,
By political groups
Supporting propositions
In return for reelection.

There was no obituary written
Although my life ended.
Nor was there a birth announcement,
Although my new life began.
Few were aware
That these changes had occurred.

Now the headlines shout again.
Read it! Read it!
Read all about it
While it's hot off the press!
It won't last long!

And my story is replaced
By another.
My story becomes old news
Fading into the archives
And only a few will remember
And know
How long my story lasts.

P.E.

I wonder why I was picked
To be timekeeper.
I'd rather be a player.

Timekeeper.

Sometime, I'll tell you about the time,
For life is all about time, isn't it?

For time immemorial
We have realized when time is up
That we have wasted time,
Thinking we had time to spare,
Time hanging on our hands.
Time after time,
That is the course of time.
We are not doing time,
This is the time of our lives.
This is how I spent my time.
What time do you have?

Just Before Suppertime

When I was very young
I would come into the kitchen,
Quietly,
On stockinged toes,
As my mother was writing a letter,
Doing the dishes,
Talking on the phone.
I would whisper,
"I am invisible
You can't see me.
You don't know I'm here."
We smiled at each other.
"What is the invisible girl doing?"
My mother wondered aloud,
Staring through the space
That was my body.
"She is climbing up on the counter,
Lifting the lid of the cookie jar,"
But my mother couldn't see me
Except if it were just before suppertime.
Invisibility never worked just before suppertime.

My mother comes into the room,
Quietly,
Like on stockinged toes.
She is out of place,
Not writing,
Not in the kitchen doing dishes,
Not talking on the phone.
She sits for hours
Not doing the ten things at once
That is my mother.
She doesn't wonder aloud.
We don't smile.

She stares at the space
That is my body.
She can't see me,
She doesn't know that I am here.
Except just before suppertime.
I can see it in her eyes then.
They focus on me,
On reality.
Each day, just before she leaves,
Just before suppertime,
I become visible.

Late at night
When colors turn invisible
And darkness permeates the eyes,
When most have escaped
Stark realities
And face only dreams,
The muffled light from the hallway
Appears as the door opens
And you come into the room
In your blue uniform,
Quietly,
As if on stockinged toes,
Pushing your dust mop around the room.
You know that I am not asleep.
You see me.
I am never invisible to you.
My body is not an empty space.
You talk to me.

"I have seen you before," you say.
"Many times.
You are the invisible girl.

There have been many invisible girls.
There will be more.
I have seen them,
Night after night.
Ghosts in bodies
With invisible minds,
Invisible thoughts.
You are here, but you are not.
I see you,
The space of your body,
But at the same time
I see nothing.
I tell them,
Each one of the invisible girls
As I visit their rooms
Mopping around the beds
Each night in the dark,
The time when ghosts
Are thought to return,
If only you would smile
They could see you.
They would know
You are here."

My mother comes into the room,
Quietly,
Like on stockinged toes,
In the hour
When ghosts lie down to sleep,
The time when she should
Be writing a letter,
Doing the dishes,
Talking on the phone.
I would whisper, if I could,

I am not invisible.
You could see me,
You know I am here.
I smile.
But she can't see.
My smile is invisible
Like me.

I am here.
I am alive.
I survived.
But you'll never see me.
I am an invisible girl.

Thoughts for My Mother

Your world was a crystal glass,
Oh, so very fragile,
And, oh, so very beautiful,
With reflections of colors
Sparkling, filled to the brim.
I am so sorry
That you watched it fall,
Could not catch it
Could not stop it
From turning into shards
Broken onto the floor.
Each shard stares up at you,
Shattered reflections,
Never whole again.
You cannot pick up the pieces,
Put them together again,
Mend this crystal glass.
There are too many fragments,
Too many slivers.
They are too sharp
And they cut deep into you
As you try.

Maybe the sands of time
Will wash upon these shards,
Buff them like sea glass,
Smooth their jagged edges,
Dull the pain of your reflections.
And, maybe,
Maybe then,
You can gather up the pieces.

Either One

The minister came today.
He said a prayer
Standing over my bedside,
Holding my hand
That could not hold back.

My mother stood on the other side.
She also held my hand.
I wish I could just squeeze,
Letting her know I was there.

They reached over the bed,
Over my stilled body.
Reached until their hands met
And held tight,
Clinging to hope,
Forming a circle.
Could it be the circle of life
Which must contain an element of death
In order for the circle to be complete?

"Dear Father,
Bless this family
Who feels the weight of human sorrow.
Help them understand
That in your infinite wisdom and love
This suffering is only
An earthly manifestation
And that you,
Our Father,
Have a greater heavenly plan
That, through the blanket of our grief,
We cannot comprehend.
Help us to realize

We are not left here alone
With our pain
But that your eternal love
Surrounds us . . ."

He prayed on.
I stopped listening
I had my own prayer.

Dear God,
Give me life
Or give me death
But do not let me lie here
Unable to have
Either one.

School Play

Our school play was different this year.
There was no script,
No practice,
No dress rehearsal.
We had only one performance,
One chance.

When we walked out on stage
The director had only one instruction—
Make it real.
We had to ad lib our parts,
Choose our direction,
Follow where things led,
Find our roles.

The curtains opened
And there we were,
All the actors mixed together,
Each finding their own path,
Each playing off each other.

The play evolved,
Became a drama,
Both a comedy
And a tragedy
In constant flux.
Some scenes ran smoothly.
Others were rough.
Accidents happened
But the play went on.
Some died on the stage.
Others survived.
Some went home unscathed,
Some lives were changed forever.

I was not a lead character,
Not a super hero
Who returned after fighting all odds,
Not one whose personal struggles
Benefited others.
I had a short and minor part.
As an actress,
I was not remembered
But my role was unforgettably haunting.

Graduation

Day merges with night,
Night merges with the past,
The past merges with the future,
Until all are one.
Nothing to distinguish
One from the other.
No graduation,
No significant degree
Of change.
All is the present.

They sit me up,
Lay me down,
Turn me over,
Turn me back.
All the while my heart beats on,
Strong and vibrant.
Its rhythm
Connects the past
And the present
And the future
As day merges with night,
Night merges with the past,
The past merges with the future.

A woman comes.
A stranger with graying hair.
She says she is my sister,
That she is here each week.
But weeks merge with months
And months merge with days
And days merge with years
And years merge with minutes
Until all are one.

The woman is nice
But she is not my sister.
My sister is a girl
Who does not come anymore.
The stranger brushes my hair,
Washes my face,
Straightens my bedclothes.
She hums and sings.
Her voice is strong and vibrant.
Its sound
Connects the past
And the present
And the future
As day merges with night,
Night merges with the past,
The past merges with the future . . .

About the Author

Judy Young is the award-winning author of twenty-nine children's poetry, fiction, and nonfiction books, including, *Promise,* a novel for middle grade and young adult readers, and *R is for Rhyme, A Poetry Alphabet* which received a starred Kirkus review, Mom's Choice Gold Award, Educators' Choice Award, Missouri Writers' Guild Best Juvenile Book Award, National Parenting Publication Association Honor Award and has been used to teach poetry writing in middle school, high school and college classrooms. Prior to writing full time, Judy was employed as a speech and language pathologist working with children and adults who suffered from traumatic brain injuries and neurological disabilities. Judy resides in the mountains in southeast Idaho with her husband, Ross, and three dogs.

Read more about Judy and her books at
www.judyyoungpoetry.com.

www.ingramcontent.com/pod-product-compliance
Lightning Source LLC
Chambersburg PA
CBHW021025090426
42738CB00007B/902